HOW TO SAY

CW00848427

WITHOUT FEELING GUILTY, HORRIBLE, SELFISH, MEAN, OR BAD

PAT CHEEKS | RN, PMHCNS-BC

Psychiatric/Mental Health Clinical Nurse Specialist, BC

225 North High Street
Harrisonburg, VA 22801
http://www.PatCheeks.com

ISBN-13: 978-1979443449
ISBN-10: 1979443440

Ordering and other information:
Quantity sales. Special discounts are available on quantity purchases by corporations, associations, and others. For details, contact the publisher at the address above.
Orders by U.S. trade bookstores and wholesalers. Please contact : Tel: (540) 908-5118; or visit www.PatCheeks.com/store.
Cover design and editing by Becky Blanton. http://beckyblanton.com

DEDICATED TO

Everyone who has ever struggled with saying "No."

"Daring to set boundaries and to say 'No,' is about having the courage to love ourselves even when we risk disappointing others."

TABLE OF CONTENTS

CHAPTER ONE

Why Is it So Hard to Just Say "No" 9

CHAPTER TWO

No is a complete sentence 13

CHAPTER THREE

No One Said It Would Be Easy,
But I Promise It Will Be Powerful 15

CHAPTER FOUR

Practice Makes Perfect...17

CHAPTER FIVE

Stay Calm and Just Say No..................................19

CHAPTER SIX

Honesty Rules...21

CHAPTER SEVEN

It's Okay to Walk Away 23

CHAPTER EIGHT

Embrace the Broken Record 27

CHAPTER NINE

Can You Hear Me Now? 29

CHAPTER TEN

Healthy Boundaries are Good Boundaries 31

CHAPTER ELEVEN

What Part of No Didn't You Understand?.............35

CHAPTER TWELVE

Holidays. The Best Time of The Year For "No."....37

CHAPTER THIRTEEN

My Life Matters 41

TABLE OF CONTENTS

CHAPTER FOURTEEN

No Doesn't Require an Explanation, Ever............43

CHAPTER FIFTEEN

Don't Say Yes Because it's Hard to Say No 49

CHAPTER SIXTEEN

Don't Mistake Kindness for Weakness 51

CHAPTER SEVENTEEN

Say It Like You Mean It 55

CHAPTER EIGHTEEN

Danger is Real. Fear is a Choice...........................57

CHAPTER NINETEEN

No Can Be Both Offensive and Defensive 61

SUMMARY 65

ABOUT PAT CHEEKS...69

CHAPTER ONE

Why is it so Hard to Just Say "No"

"Half of the troubles of this life can be traced
to saying yes too quickly, and
not saying no soon enough."

My heart went out to the woman in line in front of me at a major bookstore. The clerk was insistent on selling her a book card membership, a $25 annual fee. She clearly and confidently said, "No thanks, not today." But that only fueled the fire. Saying no to the clerk was like waving a red flag in front of a bull.

He said, "Really?" in an arrogant tone that implied she was crazy to pass up such a great deal. It rattled her. She thought for a moment, then said, "No, no, I really don't want a card today."

I think everyone in line was silently rooting for her, even though the next few exchanges showed her appear to weaken and almost cave to his insistence. She even looked in her wallet briefly for support. In spite of her obvious discomfort, he persisted. I thought I saw her about to buy a card, then she straightened her shoulders, stood up and said, strongly and while looking him in the eye, "No, I really don't want one."

The clerk looked disgusted. He said, "Well, okay, it's your loss."

She looked at him and said, "I suppose it is." She took her bags and left.

A woman behind me cheered, "Go girl!"

Despite all this, when I stepped up to buy my books, the clerk began again with his sales pitch. "Do you want to buy a book card today?"

"No thank you," I said firmly, looking him in the eye. "I don't want to buy a book card today." I felt both intimidated and empowered.

"Are you sure?" He began the same scripted aggression he had tried on the woman in front of me. I was surprised. Like the woman in front of me, I had been very clear about what I wanted — or rather, what I *didn't* want. I said no in a very strong, matter-of-fact way, and still he persisted.

I might have caved and bought a card myself if I hadn't witnessed the slender young woman in front of me stand her ground. He looked at me, looked at the long line of customers obviously upset with the exchange, and let it drop. I left feeling nervous, excited, scared, and a bit miffed.

What is it about the word "no" that makes it hard for people to hear... but harder still for people to say and then stand by it?

I've worked with sexual assault survivors, many of whom struggled with the fact that they said "no" and their dates ignored them. Had they not said it strongly enough? Were they not clear? Did they say no in a way that implied yes?

It's *hard* to say "no," especially to family and friends. None of us want to be the bad guy. We don't want to disappoint those around us. We want to please those we love and even those we work with. Many of us have grown up believing it's bad, wrong, or negative to say "no" to any request, reasonable or not.

But it's *not* bad. It's not wrong. It's not unreasonable.

"No" is the perfect answer when enforcing or communicating our boundaries. "No" helps us keep the peace. "No" lets others know what they can expect from us. It frees us to do what we need to do for ourselves.

Different people say "no" in different ways. All of them can be effective, but some work better than others.

How effective your "no" is depends on your personality, your confidence, your assertiveness, and your boundaries.

Don't worry. Saying no, setting boundaries, and being assertive are all part of the "social skills" most of us were never taught. It's never too late to learn, but all skills take practice to develop. Reading, practicing what you learn, and talking to trusted friends, a counselor, a coach, or a transition navigator can help. Even practicing in front of a mirror can do wonders!

What follows are some tips for saying "no" that my clients have told me they found very useful.

CHAPTER TWO

No is a Complete Sentence

"Don't say maybe if you want to say no."

- Anonymous

USE THE WORD "NO"

First things first: USE the actual word, "No." Don't waffle. Don't substitute a weaker phrase for the word itself. When people hear you say, "I don't think so, not today, maybe later," or "not this time," people don't hear the word, "no." They hear an invitation to argue with you, to convince you, to sell you on changing your mind.

I encourage clients to repeat the word out loud during the day so they get used to saying it and hearing it. Practice in front of a mirror. Sing along to your car radio. Do whatever makes it easier for you to get comfortable with the word!

CHAPTER THREE

No One Said It Would Be Easy,
But I Promise It Will Be Powerful

"Pay attention when people react with anger and hostility to your boundaries. You have found the edge where their respect for you ends."

- Anonymous

DON'T BE AFRAID TO REPEAT YOURSELF

I noticed something else about the woman at the counter that I see among people who successfully say no. She wasn't afraid to repeat herself, and repeat herself more than once. People, especially salespeople, work hard to convince their customers to say "yes." In the process they forget, or refuse to believe, that "no" is an answer.

People who don't respect other people's boundaries will also ignore an appropriate "no" and keep pushing.

If someone is aggressive, persistent, or ignores your "no," this doesn't mean you have to change your mind or give in to their pushiness. I tell my clients to become a broken record — to keep repeating "no" until the person gives up. If someone persists after you've repeatedly told them no, walk away, even if it means leaving your purchase at the counter. Don't be afraid to ask to speak with a manager or supervisor, either. That request, more than any other, will shut down a pushy salesperson — *fast*.

CHAPTER FOUR

Practice Makes Perfect

"Sometimes all you need is twenty seconds of insane courage, and I promise something great will come out of it." Matt Damon from movie, "We Bought a Zoo."

PRACTICE. SAY NO OFTEN AND WITH GUSTO

When I'm working with clients learning to say no, we practice saying the word a lot. We start with something easy and silly, like, "Do you want to run laps around my office while we talk?" Of course they don't. They laugh and say, "No!" Learning to say no begins with feeling comfortable with hearing yourself say it in the first place.

It's okay to say it in your head or to say it out loud. I have one client who says it to her television.

When a character asks something she herself would say no to, like, "Get in the car," or, "Drive the getaway car," she says, "No, I will not get in the car!" or "No, I will not drive the getaway car." There's no one there to hear her, but she says she really gets into it. She shouts, she laughs, and she stands up and yells sometimes. What she's doing is getting comfortable with saying no — and with hearing herself say no. Try it.

When the time comes to say "no" in a real or difficult situation, remembering yourself shouting "No! I will not clean up my room!" at the television set can give you the courage you need to act in real life.

CHAPTER FIVE

Stay Calm and Just Say No

"You can be a kind person with a good heart and still say 'No.' You can also kick butt if you need to."
- Pat Cheeks

DON'T BE A JERK

What I admired most about the woman at the bookstore was that she didn't get angry, rude, or obnoxious about her "no." The clerk was certainly rude, pushy, and aggressive, but her response to him remained the same — calm, quiet, and centered. Even as his arrogance escalated, she remained calm. She knew what so many of us don't. *She understood that we have a right to say no and to have it respected.* She had every right to say no and not feel guilty that she wasn't helping the clerk win some sales award or make his book card quota.

She didn't have to get angry to feel self-assured, although many of us do.

She didn't feel the need to meet his aggression with aggression. One of the myths I often have to dispel is that even when we do say no, and have a right to say no, some people aren't going to be happy with us. They will try to manipulate, guilt, shame, or intimidate us into changing our minds. It's up to us to decide when and where it's in our best interest to keep saying no (or to say yes).

Even though we have a right to say no, and a right not to give in to another's demands, the process and the interaction can be uncomfortable, scary, and frightening. If you're new to saying no, try to learn by refusing little requests. You can then move up to the larger, more intimidating situations.

If you find yourself getting angry, shouting, or being abusive, notice what you're doing and what you're feeling. Learn from it do better next time. This is a skill. Practicing (and failing) is part of the process.

CHAPTER SIX

Honesty Rules

"The art of leadership is saying no, not saying yes. It is very easy to say yes." - Tony Blair

BE BRIEF AND BE HONEST

There's an old expression: "Ask so-and-so the time and they'll tell you how to build a watch." It refers to someone who tends to give you more answer than you asked for.

Sometimes, when we say no to someone or they say no to us, we give or get more answer than we need. There's no reason to elaborate or provide details (true or false) about why you're saying no. Keep it short and simple. The shorter your response, the less opportunity and information your requester will have to argue you into changing your mind.

If you elaborate, you may also sound like you're lying or guilty. If you want to stay home and read a book, relax, go to a movie, or go to bed early, *just say so*. You have a right to your life. You were not put on this Earth to please everyone or to make their lives easier.

CHAPTER SEVEN

It's Okay to Walk Away

*"Sometimes when you're trying to
be everyone's anchor you fail to see
you're actually drowning instead."*
- Anonymous

DON'T BE AFRAID TO WALK AWAY

Fall is the time of year for many groups and organizations to conduct their fundraising efforts. I'm seeing Boy Scouts and other groups at storefronts selling cookies, popcorn, and Christmas wrapping paper. So are my clients!

"How can I say no to a child?" one client asked me. "He was so sweet and scared and cute. I couldn't say no to him."

Well, she could have, but she didn't. She ended up spending close to $100 on food and wrapping paper. "I don't even celebrate Christmas," she said. "And I bought it anyway."

She left the store parking lot feeling depressed and angry with herself. "I really don't want or need it, but I just couldn't say no," she said.

It's not just cute Boy Scouts, beautiful models, or charming salespeople who destroy our defenses. It's all kinds of people. It's our mothers, fathers, in-laws, and friends. It's our co-workers, clients, and colleagues. It's people we want to please.

We want to say "yes" to feel good about ourselves. The problem is not with the salesperson. It's not with whoever's asking. The problem is with us. It's that we don't know what we want.

You don't have to linger, take that free sample, or handle the items being offered. In fact, it's better if you don't. Studies show that we're hardwired to reciprocate when someone gives us something. If you eat just one hot dog or drink one can of soda from a car dealer, then look at cars, you're more likely to buy a car. I know. It sounds crazy, but it's called the "Law of Reciprocity." It's the first step down the slippery slope to buying something or doing something you don't really want to do.

I know it's hard to say no to that opportunity, or sales, or whatever, but before you get sucked in, shake your head and say, "No thanks. Not today," and walk away.

Sure, they'll be disappointed, but learning to deal with your own emotions is part of growing up.

If the person is an adult, they need to learn to accept, process, and deal with their disappointments. Other people's emotions aren't your responsibility. As long as you've been respectful and polite (what an average person would consider normal), you're fine. It's up to the Boy Scout, the salesperson, your coworker, your mother-in-law, or whomever to deal with what they're feeling. Honest. It is.

CHAPTER EIGHT

Embrace the Broken Record

"Sometimes, we need to say no to the things people want from us so that we have more time to say yes to the things they truly need from us."

- Pat Cheeks

DON'T BE AFRAID TO SAY NO OVER AND OVER AGAIN

I'm a vegetarian. Sometimes people forget. Sometimes people don't care. Sometimes people don't understand what that means. Sometimes they think I'll make an exception for them and their specialty meat dishes. (I won't!) I'm learning to tell them, "Your turkey casserole looks and smells divine, but I'm a vegetarian. I just won't ever, ever try it because, well, I'm a vegetarian for life now." I often have to say it over and over again, nicely of course. Is that okay? Yes!

Harsh? Maybe. But it's important that people understand what our boundaries are, and why we have them if that's necessary.

CHAPTER NINE

Can You Hear Me Now?

"You need to stop doing things for someone when you find out it's expected rather than appreciated."
- Pat Cheeks

USE BODY LANGUAGE

A former client of mine is Italian and proud of it. She has no trouble saying no to anyone. I asked her to tell me her secret. She told me, "I wave my arms, I shake my head, I clap my hands, then," she said, throwing her arms and hands in the air, "I say *finis*. That means the discussion is over."

You don't have to be Italian to put body language to good use. Shake your head while saying no, put your hand in front of your body, and move it side-to-side. Remember the "speak to the hand" motion of the 90s? This is body language.

Think about all the ways you've seen people say no with their bodies. Crossing your arms in front of your chest, looking down at the ground or away from the person you're talking to, holding up your hand, and turning away from the speaker are great ways to convey your "no" physically while also speaking it.

Even small children recognize when a facial expression means "no."

CHAPTER TEN

Healthy Boundaries Are Good Boundaries

"The first thing you need to learn is that the person who is angry at you for setting boundaries (and saying no), is the one with the problem."
- Drs. Cloud and Townsend from their book, Boundaries: When to Say No, How to Say Yes.

ITS CALLED HUMAN NATURE FOR A REASON

There's a lot to be said for being a Psychiatric/Mental Health Clinical Nurse Specialist. I've learned a lot of tips for turning people's psychology to my advantage when saying no. For example, honest flattery is great. I'm not the best person to give references or to write glowing accolades to students, friends, or colleagues — and I tell them so. I use the phrase, "I'm flattered," which I am.

I also tell them the truth and use the word "unfortunately" to prepare them for my no. I follow that up with something positive, such as an alternative or a barter. Sometimes, I just let it fall where it falls — at "no."

"Judy," I'll say, "I'm flattered you'd ask me for a letter of reference, but unfortunately, I'm just not a writer. I'd be happy to give you a phone reference, or sign off on a letter Dr. _____, has written, but I just can't craft the kind of letter you need."

I'm often asked to commit to things that simply would take too much of my time. I'm honored that people ask, but saying no could make me sound ungrateful. I use the words, "I'm flattered," or "I'm honored," which I truly am.

I then say "unfortunately" and explain why I can't do whatever it is. It's okay to flatter someone honestly before saying no. It can soften the blow, or acknowledge that you like the person and want to help, but just can't do what they ask. You'd be surprised how effective, appropriate, and positive this can be.

One of my clients' daughters, for example, was asked to care for her grandson, Devon, for a month while the parents "took a break" and went on a month-long, work-related vacation. My client had other, more pressing demands on her time, like a new part-time job and a new boyfriend.

She was seeing me to learn how best to transition into love, work, and grand-parenting without giving up herself. She loved her grandson but just was not ready or willing to become a full-time babysitter. This would have forced her to give up her new job and interests if only for a month (which she feared could turn into years).

We worked together to craft a "no" for her daughter. She finally told her, "I am so happy — thrilled, actually — that you're willing to trust me with Devon for a month! He is a perfect joy. Six months ago I would have said yes, but unfortunately, I now have a new job and a new boyfriend, so I need to say no. I'm flattered, but I just wouldn't have the time and energy to spend with Devon. He deserves full-time attention from a good caretaker. I'm willing to take him for one weekend, and only one weekend, while you're away, but that's all. Maybe your sisters can help you this time."

We suggested her daughter's two sisters because they were responsible, currently unemployed, and available. Her daughter was disappointed that her mother wouldn't step up to run the show, but ultimately having her sisters step in (they said yes) created a closer bond among them all.

You never know how far truth, honesty, boundaries, and being forthright with others will take you when you say "no."

Other phrases you can use are:

- "It's not possible for me right now. In fact, it's impossible."
- "Last time/last year when I did this, it was great, but I am not available this year."
- "Thank you for asking, but I'm happy with my current phone/insurance/healthcare/cable/television company, so no."
- "How thoughtful of you to offer to throw a party of 50 people for my birthday. However, I've already planned for a quiet, small dinner party of six of my old college roommates, so not this year, but thank you!"

CHAPTER ELEVEN

What Part of "No" Didn't You Understand?

"Saying no can be the ultimate self-care."
— *Claudia Black*

SAVE YOUR RUDE FOR WHEN IT MATTERS

Being rude, confrontational, or sarcastic isn't for everyone, but I have a client or two who can rock the harsh "no" if needed. I encourage them to reserve it for those times when nothing else works, as rude can be a major bridge burner and make all parties feel disrespected or upset.

That said, some of the phrases clients have come up with as alternatives to four-letter words are:

- "What part of no didn't you understand?"
- "You do realize no is a complete sentence, don't you?"
- "I just said 'no' three times. Would you understand me better if I said, 'Hell, no'?"

- No answer, just wild, maniacal laughing while shaking your head and walking away.
- "I SAID NO!" Say this in a loud, angry tone of voice after someone has ignored your more civil attempts to say no. This works for aggressive salespeople like the bookstore clerk, rude children, inebriated people, and anyone who refuses to take no for an answer.

CHAPTER TWELVE

Holidays. The Best Time of The Year For "No."

*"Anybody who gets upset or expects you to say yes
all the time clearly doesn't have
your best interest at heart."*
— *Stephanie Lahart*

THE HOLIDAYS AND "NO"

For most of us, especially women, the holidays kick off the slippery slope of saying yes when we want to say no. We don't want to disappoint, especially around the holidays. We want to care for our family, show our love, and help with all the shopping, baking, cooking, parties, and whatever comes our way.

Our inability to say "no" is what makes us frustrated, short-tempered, and anxious come Christmas.

No wonder we're so happy to see the end of the year. Our New Year's resolution is that next year we'll say "no" and mean it!

Okay. Stop. Before this holiday season gets rocking, take some time and decide now what you will and won't do this year. These are examples only; you'll need to make up your own boundaries:

- I will only throw two (or four, or whatever number YOU feel comfortable with) parties between now and New Year's.
- I will not help with any school or community holiday productions my child is not in.
- I will only go caroling one time and then only for two hours.
- I will not bake for any events where I will not be consuming the goods. I will buy cookies, etc., but I'm not baking.
- I am planning to spend Thanksgiving with family only.
- I will not host any extended family (only my children and grandchildren) in our home this Christmas.
- I will only attend one party a week.

- I will only have lunch or coffee with two people a week.

Whatever you decide to do this holiday season is up to you. If you have your boundaries in place and your calendar set, you'll find it easier to say no honestly when the requests and last-minute pleas come rolling in. You can even share this booklet with friends, family, and colleagues to let them know you're not being mean.

You're just taking care of you so you'll be able to be there for them when it truly matters. If you're a parent or have ever supervised people, you know it is easier to be strict and then loosen the reins than to be flexible and try to tighten them later. Likewise, it's easier to say "no" at first, then reconsider later.

I block out time for my walks with my dogs, to meditate, to walk the labyrinth near me, to volunteer at the homeless shelter I help with, and so on. I make sure the people, things, and projects that are important to me are protected, honored, and committed to first. Then, if there is time on my calendar and I know I'll have the energy, I'm open to other options.

Steve Jobs once said, "You have to say no to 1,000 things before you find the one thing worth saying yes to." His wisdom was in recognizing that we must focus on what we want if we're to achieve it. We have to know what we want in order to know what we *don't* want.

What follows are the nine "no's" I teach my clients. I hope they inspire and help you too. There may be some repetition of the advice above, but it never hurts to say things twice!

CHAPTER THIRTEEN

My Life Matters

"I don't say no because I am so busy and overwhelmed. I say no because I don't want to be so busy or overwhelmed." - Anonymous

THE PERFECTLY VALID NO

No matter what anyone may tell you, you never *NEED* a reason to say "no" other than that you don't want to do whatever it is someone is asking you to do. However, because we tend to feel like we should explain, most of us are uncomfortable not citing a reason for saying "no." We want a valid reason that a reasonable person would hear, respect, and honor.

I call that the "Perfectly Valid No." The perfectly valid no is a good reason, excuse, or explanation for your no.

It's something you feel will justify your no to the person(s) asking. For example, someone asks you to go out with them for the evening. You're tired. You don't want to spend time with the person. Maybe there's some other reason you don't want to go. You can make up a reason, you can be truthful, you can be apologetic, or you can offer any of a dozen perfectly valid "no" statements and leave it at that. If the person persists, become a broken record. Repeat yourself until they get the message:

- "I've been out three times this week. I'm staying home and reading books with the kids."
- "I have to work tomorrow, and I don't want to feel exhausted all day, so no thanks."
- "I'm just not feeling like it tonight. I'm not going this time."

Finally, say it like you mean it.

CHAPTER FOURTEEN

No Doesn't Require an Explanation, Ever

"Simplify your life. Learn to say no to begin with."

- Anonymous

HOW TO SAY NO AFTER YOU'VE SAID YES

We've all done it. We've all said "yes" and then regretted our decision or changed our minds. Maybe something else came up. Maybe we got sick. Maybe our situation at home or work changed, or we just decided we no longer wanted to do whatever we had agreed to. We don't want to disappoint, or back out, or not honor our obligations.

On the one hand, we feel guilty and duty-bound to honor our commitments. On the other hand, for whatever reason, we need to say no.

If you're nodding your head, ask yourself if you're a back-out-of-commitments queen.

Are you always promising to do something, then having to back out, cancel, or make excuses? Are you frequently a last-minute no-show? It's perfectly okay to back out of the occasional commitment. Things come up. If you're doing it more than once a week, however, you have a problem.

If you routinely promise and cancel on people, you'll develop a reputation for being a flip-flopper. Friends, family, an coworkers will think of you as undependable, unreliable, and untrustworthy. Learn to make "no" your go-to answer. Say no the first time, every time. If that's too hard to do right now, you can say:

"Let me check my calendar and get back with you." Or, " I can't commit right now, so no. If things change, I'll let you know."

If you think about it and then later decide you can do it, or want to do it, that's easy. It's better to say "no," then change your no to a yes, than the other way around. But if you have said "yes" and must now say no, do it quickly, as soon as you realize you need to back out.

This gives the person time to find a replacement or make other arrangements. Plus, you won't feel increasing guilt as the date approaches.

When you know you're going to make the person's task that much harder by waiting to back out, the stress on you is greater too. If you're going to back out, do it quickly, with grace and as little drama as possible.

It doesn't matter if you've agreed to something major, like being a maid of honor or the best man at a friend's wedding, or something as trivial as going dancing with friends. If you can't make it, call or text, or send an email, but say "no" as quickly as possible. Don't let the person shame, guilt, manipulate, or force you into changing your mind because you're already feeling guilty for letting them down. Write the word "NO!" down and stare at it while you talk if you have to, but say it. Here's a tried and true way to say no after you've committed yourself and must back out:

"I've made a mistake. I realized right after we spoke that I shouldn't have committed myself. I'm sorry. I'll have to back out," is a phrase many therapists are taught to use, and teach.

If the person expresses anger, regrets, sadness, distress, or whatever emotion they're feeling, acknowledge that.

Own your actions. Say:

"I know this leaves you in a bad place. I'm sorry. I made a mistake. I'm letting you know so you have time to find someone else."

Let the person know you understand what they're feeling and that you're sorry, but that you simply shouldn't have committed. If they demand an answer, an explanation, or want to know why you shouldn't have committed, you have two options. You can just say, "I made a mistake and shouldn't have committed myself. Thank you for understanding."

Alternatively, you can tell the truth. "It sounded great, but I thought about it, and I would just rather stay home and chill that weekend."

You will be tempted to tell a lie, even a little white lie, to sound more convincing and to make your excuse sound stronger. Don't do it. Honesty is always the best policy. People will know if you're lying and will respect you more if you tell the truth — no matter how lame it may sound. If you back out and the person says, "You're always doing this," then listen to them. Maybe they're right. Maybe you have a hard time saying "no" and it's starting to impact your relationships.

After you've said no, hang up the phone and breathe a huge sigh of relief. Remember the stress. Remember that feeling of having to own up and back out.

Remember it next time you're thinking about leaping into saying "yes" before thinking things through. The person may not be happy or may distance themselves from you, but if they're a good friend, they'll come back. That is, they'll come back unless you're a flake and you do this a lot. It feels good to please someone by saying "yes," but if you can't follow through, that's another issue.

CHAPTER FIFTEEN

Don't Say Yes Because it's Hard to Say No

"People learn how to treat you based on what you accept from them." — *Anonymous*

THE "I KNOW I DID IT BEFORE, BUT I CAN'T DO IT NOW" NO

How many of you have done something for years, whether it's volunteering for something, being a coach for your child's school soccer team, or simply hosting all the neighborhood baby showers? Have you been the go-to guy or gal people depend on?

What happens when you decide not to be that person anymore because you have grown, changed, lost interest, or just don't want to commit to something every year?

You say "no." You say, "Guys, I've loved every year I've participated in this, but I'm moving on to other commitments and will not be doing it this year. I'm flattered you're asking, but no. I won't be able to help."

When we are someone who makes other people's lives easier, they're not going to let us go without a struggle. They may ask several times, in various ways. They may recruit others to ask you as well, hoping someone will have the leverage to convince you to change your mind.

This is the kind of situation you can expect, with multiple people pressuring you. No one wants to lose a team player, a person who has always been dependable and good, or even who just showed up every year.

Be prepared to say, "I'm very sure about this. I know I did this before, but I can't do it now. Please spread the word that while I'm honored and flattered, I'm not doing it this year."

CHAPTER SIXTEEN

"Don't mistake kindness for weakness."

"You can be a good person with a kind and generous heart, a great love for all mankind, and still say no. Wait. Actually, you can't be all those things unless you can say no." - Anonymous

THE POLITE NO

The one thing I hear from police officers I've worked with in the past, and from rape and crime survivors, is that they regret not taking action sooner. They "felt" something was off, or that the man on the elevator, or in the parking lot, had ill intentions toward them, but that they didn't want to "offend" the man by appearing rude. They didn't want to get off the elevator after he got on. They didn't want to tell the man groping them on the subway to stop or back off.

They didn't want to brandish their mace or pepper spray because they were taught to be polite.

Fear of offending a perpetrator gets thousands of women killed every year. Others get beaten or crippled because they didn't want to seem rude. Why are we so insistent on being polite, especially when it's not in our interest to do so?

Saying no to someone in an empty parking garage or elevator is one thing, but why are we equally apprehensive to say no to a pushy colleague or co-worker? We fear offending. We put other people's needs and wants ahead of our own — in unhealthy ways.

The one thing I hear from the majority of my female clients is that they want to be polite, to be professional, and not to offend. That's fine. But that fear of not appearing polite or professional, or of not offending, can keep us from ever saying "no," even when it *is* appropriate.

I'm asking you to consider when, why, where, and how to be polite — and what to do when polite is no longer an option. When we understand when, where, and why we need to be polite, it's easier to do so because we feel confidence in our decision. Being polite is more than not offending. It's showing respect for the person and their request while honoring your own needs.

For example:

"I'm sorry, but my schedule doesn't permit me to take on any more obligations right now." You've been polite, honest, and to the point. Many people will respect your polite no, but many will not.

There's a line between being a likable person and being a people pleaser. Learning how to navigate those rocky waters can be challenging. Some polite ways to say no include:

- "Let me think about it." This is a polite way of giving yourself time to consider a request without committing to it before you know what you're agreeing to. Your request for more time is professional, polite, and reasonable. Any demand for an immediate answer from the requestor is not. If you are pressed for an immediate commitment, simply repeat your answer: "I need time to think about it. I can't give you an answer today."

- "I'll need to check with my supervisor, boss, spouse, neighbor, manager, etc." Not only does this let the person know you're taking him/her seriously, but that you're respecting the times/demands of others.

Deferring an answer by saying, "I'm honored, flattered, or humbled that you'd ask," is not offensive at all.

It's a very polite way of acknowledging the honor you feel at being asked to clean up, collecting beer-soaked party cups and empty trash after the office Christmas party, while knowing all the while your next response is going to be, "Unfortunately, I have other plans that night."

Don't be afraid to redirect the questioner. "I'm flattered you'd ask, but unfortunately, I have other plans that night. Have you thought about asking Jessica?" Point the person in the direction of someone you believe would honestly appreciate the opportunity.

The art of the polite "no" mostly revolves around maintaining your cool, being professional, and giving honest but clear "no" responses when asked to do something you don't want to do.

And if that person continues to ask? Then they are being toxic, abusive, and disrespectful and it's okay to be more direct, pointed, or to even just walk away. You have a right to say no, and mean it.

CHAPTER SEVENTEEN

Say It Like You Mean It

"Saying 'no' might make other people angry, but it will make you free." - Anonymous

THE "NO WAY!" NO

The "No way!" no is for the teenage son/daughter who wants you to call your friends for a ride so he/she can have the car. Look directly in their eyes, smile, enunciate clearly, and say "No way!"

The "No way!" no is for the people who obviously want to manipulate, use, or abuse their relationship with you to get what they want. It may be family wanting to borrow money or resources they know you don't want to loan.

The person usually knows you'll say "no," but they ask anyway, hoping to catch you in a weak or generous moment.

Think carefully before saying yes to any of these requests. A single yes will encourage them to repeat their request in the future. How you let people treat you teaches them how they *CAN* treat you.

When we are inconsistent with our no's, or our boundaries, or our actions people will assume our minds can be changed. No matter how hard it is to say no, keep saying saying it. Don't be pressured, guilted or manipulated into changing your mind. Remember. Embrace the broken record.

CHAPTER EIGHTEEN
Danger is Real. Fear is a Choice.

"The difference between very successful, happy people and happy people is that very successful people say 'no' to almost everything." - *Warren Buffett*

THE COWARDLY NO

When my children were in high school, years and years ago, my husband and I gave them permission to make us the bad guys. They would say something like, "No, I can't do drugs because my parents would kill me, or sell my car, or both." If they felt peer pressure to do something where saying no would have been the right but uncool thing to do, they could blame us for their refusal.

This works great for kids being pressured or bullied at school, or teens who want to say no to drugs or sex, but who don't quite have the strength yet to do so.

As a married couple we have often said, "No, I can't do anything without checking with my spouse first." We do respect each other's calendars, but saying so is also a great way to demur when feeling pressured to do something you know you don't want to do.

Have you ever felt backed into a corner? Have you felt low on energy, courage, or both? Have you felt desperate? Use this one: "My husband/mother/child/coach doesn't want me to do that." Yep. Make someone else the "bad guy" even if you're too old to blame your parents.

I have a single client who is also a businesswoman. She is frequently asked to go, do, or participate in conferences she just doesn't have the energy or finances to attend. She says, "My accountant," or "My office manager," or "My agent," as appropriate when people won't take no for an answer. Then the person "saying no" is an administrative staff person who has no problem explaining her boss is booked and unavailable.

There comes a time when we all need to stand up and say no because we own responsibility for our decisions — including the decision to say no. The cowardly no is like training wheels. It supports our children and it can support us.

I had a client who was absolutely terrified to say no to her clients. She was a consultant and believed that telling her clients no would make them angry and make them leave. We were still working on boundaries and how to create and set them.

One day she came in after having been shopping. She had tried to return a dress and instead of the clerk saying "No, you can't return this dress," she said, "We have a policy about returns." Then she told my client what her options were. She also said, "I think it's crazy too. You never wore the dress, it has the tags on it, and we should take it back, but my hands are tied. It's just this new policy."

My client kept hearing, "new policy," while feeling like the clerk did want to help her. She came to me and said, "What if I implement new policies instead of boundaries. That's kind of like a cowardly no, right?"

It was! I loved it. Making something a policy implies that others, often more savvy and smarter than you, have decided this. It's a group thing.

One of the most telling incidents for my client was when her 8-year-old answered the kitchen phone at the dinner table one night. The child said, "My parents have a new policy about phone calls at dinner. We can't take them.

"I'll call you back later." He'd heard his mom, my client, discussing her new policies for her business and took them to heart!

Whatever you call them, finding ways to say "no" to protect ourselves, our time, our relationships, and our resources is critical. It will keep us from feeling stressed, resentful, and angry. Science proves that it will keep us healthier, too.

CHAPTER NINETEEN

No Can Be Both Offensive and Defensive

"It's easy to say 'No,"
when your goals and priorities are in order."
- Pat Cheeks

THE ABSOLUTE NO

I carry pepper spray and self-defense options with me when I travel because, well, I just never know when I'll need them. I practice with them, am not afraid of using them, and just hope I never have to deploy them. The Absolute No is like that. You need it for your protection. You hope you never have to use it, but you have it there in your mind and heart.

Absolute no statements are sentences like these:

"I will not rob this store. I will not drink and drive. I will not get in a car as a passenger with someone who is drinking and driving. I will not experiment with drugs.

I will not have sex with my unconscious friend. I will not violate my faith, conscience, religion or beliefs to impress someone at the expense of another."

The absolute no is exactly what it sounds like. It is an utter refusal with no alternatives. It's a deal-breaker. It is a strong, no-holds-barred negative in response to something so obviously wrong, risky, immoral, or insane that it should be obvious there is no other answer.

If you don't know what your absolute "no" is, you should think about it. I know of a professional at an accounting firm who discovered her boss was keeping two sets of books. He expected her to not only to keep his secret, but to cover for him. Her response was immediate.

"No!" she said, and quit her job. She also reported his secret and went through some tough financial times as he threatened her and tried to slander her name. Her records and journal ultimately proved her innocence.

She got a new, better job with an honest firm whose management was impressed by her fight and her integrity.

I'm not sure why so many of us believe that doing the right thing, acting the right way, or saying the right things will cause others to see us as heroes. It might, but more often than not, people see the "truth" through a lens biased by their own beliefs. Given the same facts, the same evidence, human nature tells us that people will still insist on seeing things differently. That's why it's so important for you to know your boundaries, to know what you want and don't want, and for you to be able to say "no" based on what's important to you.

The other thing I want to leave you with is to ask you to start thinking about boundaries — what they are, why they matter, and how to create, communicate, and enforce them. When you can do that, when you can say "no" in healthy ways, your life will improve 200%.

It won't be easy. It won't happen overnight. I guarantee, however, that your life will become better for it.

SUMMARY

"Compassionate people ask for what they need. They say no when they need to, and when they say yes, they mean it." - Brene Brown, Rising Strong

There are hundreds of books and articles online and in your favorite magazines about how to say "no" and how to set boundaries. They all have something to offer, but what they *can't* do is force you to practice until you get it right.

That's something to which you must commit. Practice with a friend or family member you trust. Find a mentor, counselor, or transitions navigator or coach to help you practice. Practicing with someone, or even speaking into a tape recorder, gives you the feedback you need to make changes. You can adjust your tone of voice and words as needed.

Feeling embarrassed about practicing a new skill, particularly a verbal one, is normal. The more you practice, the more at ease you'll feel.

If you can't find a friend, practice saying "no," to store clerks and strangers. Go into a store and, when the clerk asks, "Do you need help finding anything?" say, "Thank you, but no. I'm fine."

We all say no every day in ways we don't think about. When a waiter or waitress asks us if we'd like a refill or desert, we say "no." When our children ask if they can do something we don't want them doing — whether going out on a weekday evening or to a concert or movie we don't want them to see — we say no.

Think about the last time you said no to someone for any reason. How did it feel? How did they react? When we start realizing that we can have more, do more, feel better, and improve the lives of those around us by saying no, it gets easier.

Most people see a change in their lives within a few weeks of consistently saying "no" to the things they don't want — and *yes* to the things they *do* want.

If you'd like to learn more about how I help clients create, set and enforce their boundaries, or learn to say "no," contact me at pat@PatCheeks.com, or visit my website at http://patcheeks.com.

ABOUT PAT CHEEKS

"Saying no means you know your limits, not that you're being mean, ugly, or rude. You're saying 'Yes!' to yourself and that matters more than anything. You can't give from a place where you are depleted of anything to give."

– Pat Cheeks

Pat Cheeks is a Psychiatric/Mental Health Nurse, Board Certified. (PMHCNS-BC)

Her background includes a Master's degree in Psychiatric/Mental Health Nursing in inpatient, intensive outpatient and private practice settings.

She's also volunteered in classrooms and worked on committees for preschool, elementary, middle, high schools and college helping with different challenges facing parents, teachers and school boards as well as sports staffs.

She's volunteered with the Sexual Assault Resource Agency and Shelter for Help in Emergency (SARA and SHE) to help rape and assault victims transition from trauma back into life. An avid outdoors-woman, hiker, and camper, Pat has helped in clean ups on local trails and rivers because she believes that nature and the world and our caring for it is important.

As the mother of two now grown children, she's been through pregnancy on both sides – as one who experienced the joys and challenges; and as a nurse as well. She's taught prenatal and postpartum exercise and childbirth classes and acted as doula.

Drawing on her experiences in a variety of hospital, trauma and care settings, she's also lectured for police, teachers, health care practitioners and the public on a variety of health topics.

As a Women's Midlife Services Coordinator at one hospital, Pat worked with women and their children and partners on a variety of issues- developmental issues, starting menstrual period, perimenopause, menopause and all of the symptoms, preparing to leave for college, preparing for leaving home for new life- work, marriage, etc. empty nest, infertility, pregnancy, new baby, toddler struggles, pre-teen and teenager angst, "sandwich generation" issues, esp. caretaking, divorce, remarriage, loss, including preparing for death.

Pat has been a therapist, and unlike many life coaches she has the medical background and credentials to recognize medical and health based challenges that require therapeutic counseling or medical intervention.

Not all of us are hurting because we just had a bad day or a bad year. Sometimes there are other things going on that require a doctor's intervention. Pat can recognize the difference and offer alternatives and solutions for people who aren't sure if they want a therapist or a coach.

We all go through transitions, some with more or less ease than others. Some transitions are easier, and less stressful if you have someone to go through them with you.

Pat also specializes in working with people going through some of life's hardest transitions:

- Pregnancy
- New Parenting
- Marital Issues
- Divorce
- Recent Illness Diagnosis
- Spiritual Crisis
- Impending Death – of a Loved One or Self
- Grief

Our bodies may age, but our souls are timeless. Our bodies store the traumas that we have experienced since we were in the womb. You can free the trauma, understand it where needed, and work with it to learn the lessons it can teach you. Pat encourages clients to listen to the messages, subtle and not so subtle, that you receive from yourself during your transition work to ensure you have a healthier life, more life coping skills, and greater insight and awareness into yourself.

Contact Pat for more information:

Pat@PatCheeks.com
http://patcheeks.com

Printed in Great Britain
by Amazon